Darius Rucker

DARIUS RUCKER

THE LIFE FROM BEGINNING TO THE END

FACT PUBLISHER

Darius Rucker Life Story

Copyright © 2024 FACT PUBLISHER

All rights reserved.

No part of this publication may be reproduced, distributed, or transmitted in any form or by any means, including photocopying, recording, or other electronic or mechanical methods, without the prior written permission of the publisher, except as permitted by U.S. copyright law.

Darius Rucker Life Story

TABLE OF CONTENTS

INTRODUCTION	2
PART I	6
EARLY LIFE AND CAREER BEGINNINGS	6
Chapter 1: Growing Up In Charleston	6
Chapter 2: Formation Of Hootie & The Blowfish Formation Of Hootie & The Blowfish	17
PART II	27
THE HOOTIE & THE BLOWFISH ERA	27
Chapter 3: Rise to Fame	27
Chapter 4: Balancing Success And Personal Life	37
Chapter 5: Beyond the Hits	46
PART III	55
SOLO CAREER AND COUNTRY MUSIC	55
Chapter 6: The Decision To Go Solo	55
Chapter 7: Breaking Into Country Music	63
Chapter 8: Country Music Success	72
PART IV	79
BEYOND THE MUSIC	79
Chapter 9: Philanthropy And Activism	79
Chapter 10: Business Ventures And Other Interests	87
Chapter 11: Legacy And Impact	95
CONCLUSION	**99**

Darius Rucker Life Story

INTRODUCTION

Darius Rucker: From Charleston to Country Stardom

In the tapestry of American music, few artists have navigated such a dramatic and successful shift in genre as Darius Rucker.

Born and raised in the vibrant city of Charleston, South Carolina, his journey from the soulful frontman of the rock band Hootie & the Blowfish to a chart-topping country music superstar is a testament to both raw talent and unwavering determination.

Rucker's story is one of unlikely triumphs and unexpected turns. Growing up in a close-knit African American community, he was immersed in a rich musical culture that would shape his artistic identity.

From the gospel hymns echoing through the local churches to the rhythm and blues that pulsated through the city's streets, music was an integral part of his life. It was during his college years at the University of South Carolina that Rucker's musical path began to take shape.

Darius Rucker Life Story

Teaming up with fellow students, he formed Hootie & the Blowfish, a band that would defy expectations and capture the hearts of millions.

With their breakthrough album, "Cracked Rear View," Hootie & the Blowfish became a cultural phenomenon, selling millions of copies and producing a string of unforgettable hits. Rucker's distinctive voice and the band's infectious blend of rock, pop, and folk music resonated with audiences across the country. For years, they reigned as one of the most popular bands in America, filling stadiums and headlining festivals.

However, beneath the glitz and glamor of stardom, Rucker yearned for a new musical challenge. The desire to explore different artistic avenues led him to make a bold decision: to leave Hootie & the Blowfish and embark on a solo career in country music.

A genre traditionally dominated by white artists, Rucker's venture into the country was met with skepticism by some. But with unwavering belief in his talent and a deep connection to the storytelling tradition of country music, he defied the odds once again.

Rucker's transition to country music was nothing short of remarkable. He seamlessly blended his soulful vocals with the heartfelt lyrics and infectious melodies of the genre, creating a sound that was both authentic and innovative. With hits like "Don't," "Wagon Wheel," and "Come Back Song," he not only captured the hearts of country music fans but also expanded the genre's audience.

This biography delves deep into the life and career of Darius Rucker, exploring the pivotal moments that shaped his journey. From his humble beginnings in Charleston to his meteoric rise to fame with Hootie & the Blowfish and his subsequent reinvention as a country music icon, we will examine the challenges, triumphs, and personal growth that have defined his extraordinary career.

We will explore the man behind the music, uncovering the passions, values, and philanthropic endeavors that have made him a beloved figure in the entertainment industry. We will also examine the impact of his music on popular culture, and how he has inspired and empowered countless fans through his authentic voice and unwavering spirit.

Ultimately, this biography seeks to capture the essence of Darius Rucker: a gifted musician, a resilient artist, and a true American original.

PART I

EARLY LIFE AND CAREER BEGINNINGS

Chapter 1: Growing Up In Charleston

The rhythmic pulse of Charleston, South Carolina, seeped into Darius Rucker's soul from the moment he drew his first breath. Born and raised in the city's vibrant tapestry, he was a product of its rich history, soulful music, and resilient spirit.

Charleston, with its cobblestone streets and grand antebellum homes, was more than just a place; it was a living, breathing entity that nurtured the young boy who would one day captivate millions with his voice.

Rucker's childhood was steeped in the traditions of the African American community that thrived in the city's heart. The melodies of gospel filled the air, their harmonies weaving through the fabric of his days.

Church was a sanctuary, a place where he found solace, inspiration, and a deep-rooted sense of community. The power of those voices, raised in praise, left an indelible mark on the young Rucker, shaping his musical sensibilities and laying the foundation for the soulful expression that would become his hallmark.

Beyond the spiritual realm, Charleston's music scene was a melting pot of influences. The city's rich history as a port city brought together people from diverse backgrounds, and their musical traditions converged to create a unique and vibrant sound.

Rucker was exposed to a myriad of genres, from jazz and blues to rhythm and blues and rock and roll. The city's juke joints and nightclubs became his musical playgrounds, where he absorbed the raw energy and soulful expression of the local musicians.

Growing up in Charleston during the civil rights era, Rucker experienced firsthand the challenges and triumphs of a community striving for equality. The city's history of racial tension and segregation was a stark reality, but it also fostered a sense of resilience and determination among its African American residents. Rucker witnessed the courage and strength of his community as they fought for justice and equality, and these experiences shaped his worldview and fueled his desire to use his platform to make a difference.

Charleston's natural beauty also played a significant role in Rucker's formative years. The city's stunning beaches, lush gardens, and historic architecture provided a backdrop for countless childhood memories.
The ocean, with its vastness and mystery, inspired a sense of wonder and adventure in the young boy. These early experiences in nature fostered a deep appreciation for the natural world and a connection to something larger than himself.

As Rucker matured, his love for music grew stronger. He began playing guitar and forming bands with his friends, exploring different genres and honing his songwriting skills.

Charleston's supportive music scene provided a fertile ground for young musicians to develop their craft, and Rucker thrived in this creative environment. The city's embrace of music and the arts instilled in him a belief in the power of music to connect people and inspire change.

Looking back, it is clear that Charleston was the crucible in which Darius Rucker's talent was forged. The city's rich cultural heritage, its vibrant music scene, and its resilient spirit provided the foundation for his extraordinary journey. As he would later discover, the world was ready for his unique blend of soul, rock, and country, but it was in the heart of Charleston that the seeds of his success were first sown.

Early Influences And Musical Beginnings

The seeds of Darius Rucker's musical journey were sown deep in the fertile soil of his Charleston upbringing. A city steeped in history, culture, and a rich tapestry of sound, it was an environment that nurtured his innate talent and ignited a lifelong passion for music.

Gospel music, with its soaring vocals and heartfelt lyrics, served as the bedrock of Rucker's musical foundation. The church was a sanctuary where he found solace and inspiration, and the power of the choir, voices united in worship, left an indelible mark on his young soul. The rhythmic pulse of gospel, its ability to evoke raw emotion and spiritual connection, became a fundamental element of his musical vocabulary.

Beyond the sacred, Charleston's vibrant music scene offered a kaleidoscope of influences. The city's historic role as a port city had brought together people from diverse cultures, resulting in a unique blend of musical styles.

Rucker was exposed to the raw energy of blues, the soulful rhythms of jazz, and the infectious grooves of rhythm and blues. These genres, with their emphasis on improvisation, storytelling, and emotional expression, resonated deeply with him.

A pivotal moment arrived when Rucker picked up a guitar. The instrument became an extension of himself, a vessel through which he could pour out his emotions and tell his stories.

Hours were spent practicing, experimenting with chords and melodies, and discovering the endless possibilities of music. The guitar became his constant companion, a source of solace and inspiration.

Rucker's early musical explorations were fueled by a relentless curiosity. He devoured records, immersing himself in the works of musical legends. From the soulful crooning of Otis Redding to the raw power of Jimi Hendrix, he sought out artists who pushed boundaries and challenged conventions. These influences expanded his musical horizons and ignited a desire to create his own unique sound.

As a young man, Rucker formed bands with friends, sharing a common love of music and a dream of making it big. They played countless gigs, honing their craft and building a local following. The experience of performing live was exhilarating, and it reinforced Rucker's belief in the power of music to connect with people on a profound level.

While these early years were marked by experimentation and exploration, a consistent thread ran through Rucker's musical journey: a deep-seated desire to communicate and connect.

Whether it was through the soaring melodies of gospel or the raw emotion of blues, he sought to create music that resonated with people on a personal level. This innate ability to connect with audiences would become one of the hallmarks of his career.

Family background and upbringing

Darius Rucker's life unfolded against the vibrant backdrop of Charleston, South Carolina, a city steeped in history, music, and the enduring spirit of its people. His family, a cornerstone of his early years, instilled in him the values, resilience, and love that would shape his character and fuel his aspirations.

Rucker's childhood was marked by a strong sense of community. Raised in a close-knit African American neighborhood, he was surrounded by extended family, neighbors, and friends who formed a supportive network.

The shared experiences, laughter, and challenges forged deep bonds that would last a lifetime.
His mother, a steadfast and loving figure, played a pivotal role in Rucker's upbringing. Balancing the demands of raising a family with her nursing career, she instilled in her children the importance of education,

hard work, and perseverance. Her unwavering belief in Rucker's talents and dreams served as a constant source of encouragement.

Music was woven into the fabric of Rucker's family life. His mother, an admirer of soul music, introduced him to the rich sounds of Al Green and Betty Wright. These artists, with their soulful voices and heartfelt lyrics, captivated the young Rucker, igniting a passion for music that would shape his future.

Despite facing economic challenges, Rucker's family prioritized education. They understood the power of knowledge and the opportunities it could unlock. Rucker excelled in school, demonstrating a thirst for learning and a natural curiosity about the world around him.

The church was another influential force in Rucker's life. The spiritual community provided a sense of belonging, fostering his faith and introducing him to the power of gospel music. The choir, with its harmonious blend of voices, resonated with his soul, inspiring him to sing and dream of performing on a larger stage.

Rucker's upbringing was marked by both joy and hardship. He experienced the warmth of family, the support of a close-knit community, and the challenges of growing up in a world with limited opportunities. Yet, it was these experiences that forged his character, building resilience, determination, and a deep appreciation for the blessings in his life.

Chapter 2: Formation Of Hootie & The Blowfish Formation Of Hootie & The Blowfish

The genesis of Hootie & the Blowfish, the band that would catapult Darius Rucker to stardom, lies within the vibrant tapestry of college life. At the University of South Carolina, a shared love for music brought together a group of friends who would embark on a musical journey that would change their lives forever.

Rucker, with his soulful voice and burgeoning songwriting talent, formed the core of the band. He was joined by Mark Bryan, a guitarist with a penchant for crafting infectious melodies, and Dean Felber, a bassist with a steady rhythmic foundation. The trio, united by a shared passion, began playing together, honing their craft and dreaming of bigger things.

The addition of Jim Sonefeld, a drummer with a rock-solid beat, completed the lineup. The four friends, bound by their musical chemistry and a desire to make their mark, embraced the name Hootie & the Blowfish, a moniker as quirky and unconventional as their sound.

The early days of Hootie & the Blowfish were marked by endless hours of practice, gigging at local bars and college campuses, and the relentless pursuit of their musical vision. They experimented with different styles, blending elements of rock, pop, and folk into a unique sound that resonated with their generation.

The band's music was characterized by catchy melodies, heartfelt lyrics, and a sense of camaraderie that was infectious. Rucker's soulful vocals, combined with Bryan's melodic guitar riffs, created a signature sound that set them apart from their contemporaries. Their music spoke to the experiences and aspirations of young people, capturing the essence of college life and the search for meaning and purpose.

As Hootie & the Blowfish gained popularity on the local scene, they began to attract the attention of music industry insiders. Their raw energy and undeniable talent caught the eye of a record label executive, leading to a life-changing record deal. With the support of a major label, the band was poised to take their music to a wider audience.

The road to success was not without its challenges. Balancing the demands of college life, band commitments, and the pressures of the music industry was no easy feat. The band members faced personal and professional obstacles, but their unwavering friendship and dedication to their music kept them united.

Despite the hurdles, Hootie & the Blowfish persevered, their determination fueled by a shared dream of making a lasting impact. They poured their hearts and souls into their music, creating songs that resonated with a growing fan base. With each performance, they honed their craft, building a reputation as a live act that could electrify an audience.

The Band's Formation And Early Struggles

The genesis of Hootie & the Blowfish lay nestled within the vibrant tapestry of college life at the University of South Carolina. A shared passion for music ignited a spark among a group of friends, destined to forge an enduring bond and create a sound that would resonate with millions.

Darius Rucker, the band's charismatic frontman, brought his soulful voice and burgeoning songwriting talent to the table. Mark Bryan, a guitarist with an uncanny knack for crafting infectious melodies, complemented Rucker's vision. Dean Felber, the steady heartbeat of the group, provided the rhythmic foundation on bass. And Jim Sonefeld, the drummer, brought a rock-solid groove to complete the musical puzzle.

Together, they formed a quartet that transcended the typical college band. Their shared dream of making music that mattered fueled their relentless pursuit of perfection. Hours were spent in cramped practice spaces, their dedication unwavering as they experimented with different sounds and styles. The band's early performances were a crucible, testing their mettle and refining their craft.

The road to musical success was far from smooth. Balancing the demands of college life, part-time jobs, and the pursuit of a music career was a formidable challenge.

Financial constraints were a constant companion, forcing them to make tough choices and sacrifices. The allure of a traditional career path often beckoned, but the magnetic pull of music kept them grounded.

Despite these hurdles, the band's camaraderie proved to be an invaluable asset. Their unwavering belief in each other fueled their determination to succeed. They supported one another through setbacks, offering encouragement and constructive criticism. Their shared vision provided a compass, guiding them through the stormy waters of the music industry.

The early years were marked by countless hours spent in dingy bars and college campuses, playing to indifferent crowds. Rejection was a frequent visitor, but the band refused to be discouraged. They learned to embrace the challenges, viewing each performance as an opportunity to grow and improve.

With each gig, Hootie & the Blowfish honed their craft, developing a unique sound that blended elements of rock, pop, and folk. Rucker's soulful vocals, combined with Bryan's melodic guitar riffs, created a captivating alchemy that resonated with audiences. The band's infectious energy and genuine connection with their fans began to set them apart from the crowd.

As their reputation grew, so did their determination to make a lasting impact. The dream of breaking out of the local scene and reaching a wider audience became an obsession. They poured their hearts and souls into their music, writing songs that reflected their experiences and aspirations.

Breakthrough With "Cracked Rear View

The release of Hootie & the Blowfish's debut album, "Cracked Rear View," was a seismic event that irrevocably altered the trajectory of the band's career. It was a moment of seismic shift, transforming them from a promising college band into a cultural phenomenon.

The album, a collection of raw, heartfelt songs that resonated with the experiences of a generation, struck a chord with audiences across the country. The infectious melodies, coupled with Darius Rucker's soulful vocals, created a sound that was both familiar and undeniably fresh. Tracks like "Hold My Hand," "Only Wanna Be with You," and "Let Her Cry" became instant classics, their lyrics capturing the complexities of love, loss, and the search for meaning.

The album's success was a testament to the band's unwavering belief in their music. Years of relentless touring, honing their craft in small clubs and college campuses, had prepared them for this moment. The hard work, the sacrifices, and the unwavering support from friends and family had all culminated in this extraordinary breakthrough.

With each passing week, "Cracked Rear View" climbed the charts, defying expectations and shattering records. The album's meteoric rise was a testament to the power of word-of-mouth, as fans shared their love for the music with friends and family. The band found themselves catapulted into the spotlight, their faces gracing the covers of magazines and their songs dominating the airwaves.

The overwhelming success of the album came with its own set of challenges. The band was thrust into a world of constant media attention, demanding schedules, and the pressure to replicate their initial success. The intense scrutiny and the demands of fame tested the bonds of friendship, but the band's shared vision and determination helped them navigate the turbulent waters of stardom.

"Cracked Rear View" was more than just an album; it was a cultural touchstone that defined a generation. The music resonated with young people who were searching for connection, meaning, and a sense of belonging. The band became a symbol of hope and possibility, inspiring countless aspiring musicians to pursue their dreams.

As the album's success continued to soar, Hootie & the Blowfish found themselves embarking on a whirlwind tour that took them across the country. The energy and excitement of the live shows were electric, as fans flocked to see the band perform their beloved songs. The experience of connecting with their audience on such a profound level was both exhilarating and humbling.

PART II

THE HOOTIE & THE BLOWFISH ERA

Chapter 3: Rise to Fame

The release of "Cracked Rear View" was a watershed moment for Hootie & the Blowfish, propelling them from relative obscurity to the pinnacle of pop stardom. The album's meteoric rise was a testament to the band's raw talent, infectious energy, and the undeniable connection they forged with their audience.

With each passing week, the album's sales soared, shattering records and capturing the attention of the music industry. The band found themselves in the unfamiliar territory of superstardom, their faces plastered on magazine covers and their music dominating the airwaves. The once-quiet existence of college life was replaced by a whirlwind of travel, interviews, and public appearances.

The band's meteoric ascent was accompanied by a tidal wave of media attention. The spotlight, while initially thrilling, also brought with it a host of challenges. The intense scrutiny of their personal lives, the constant pressure to deliver hit after hit, and the demands of a relentless touring schedule tested the bonds of friendship and the band's resilience.

Yet, amidst the chaos, Hootie & the Blowfish remained grounded by their shared love of music. They embraced the opportunity to connect with fans on a deeper level, pouring their hearts and souls into their live performances. The energy and excitement of their concerts were electric, as fans flocked to see the band bring their beloved songs to life.

The band's success extended beyond the music industry. Their infectious optimism and down-to-earth personalities made them beloved by fans of all ages. They became ambassadors for their hometown of Charleston, South Carolina, shining a spotlight on the city's rich culture and history.

As their fame grew, so did the band's philanthropic endeavors. They established the Hootie & the Blowfish Foundation, dedicated to supporting education and other charitable causes. Their commitment to giving back to their community became a hallmark of their career, inspiring countless fans to get involved in charitable work.

The journey to the top was not without its challenges, but Hootie & the Blowfish emerged as one of the most successful bands of the 1990s. Their music touched the lives of millions, creating a lasting legacy that continues to resonate today.

The Impact Of "Cracked Rear View"

The release of Hootie & the Blowfish's debut album, "Cracked Rear View," was nothing short of a cultural phenomenon. It was a sonic earthquake that shook the music industry to its core, leaving an indelible mark on popular culture. The album's impact extended far beyond record sales and chart positions, resonating deeply with a generation of listeners and reshaping the landscape of contemporary music.

At its core, "Cracked Rear View" captured the essence of youthful longing, heartbreak, and the search for meaning. Its relatable lyrics, coupled with infectious melodies, struck a chord with millions of young people who were navigating the complexities of life and love. The album provided a soundtrack for their experiences, offering solace, companionship, and a sense of belonging.

The album's success was a catalyst for a broader cultural shift. It marked the rise of a new generation of artists who embraced authenticity and storytelling over manufactured pop. Hootie & the Blowfish paved the way for a wave of singer-songwriter-driven bands that dominated the charts in the mid-1990s.

Beyond its musical impact, "Cracked Rear View" also had a profound influence on the music industry. The album's unprecedented success demonstrated the power of word-of-mouth marketing and the importance of connecting with audiences on a personal level. It challenged the traditional methods of promoting music, forcing record labels to rethink their strategies.

The album's legacy extends far beyond its initial release. Its songs have become timeless classics, continuing to be played on radio stations and enjoyed by new generations of fans. The album's enduring popularity is a testament to its quality and the deep connection it forged with listeners.

Moreover, "Cracked Rear View" played a pivotal role in shaping the careers of its creators. It launched Hootie & the Blowfish into the stratosphere of stardom, providing them with a platform to share their music with the world. The album's success afforded them the opportunity to give back to their community through philanthropic endeavors, leaving a lasting positive impact.

"Cracked Rear View" was more than just an album; it was a cultural touchstone that defined a generation. Its impact reverberated through the music industry, inspiring countless artists and reshaping the way music was consumed and experienced. The album's enduring legacy serves as a testament to its power and the profound connection it forged with millions of fans.

Touring And The Band's Popularity

The release of "Cracked Rear View" catapulted Hootie & the Blowfish into a realm of unprecedented popularity. With the album's meteoric rise, the band found themselves thrust into an endless cycle of touring, performing their songs for adoring fans across the country. The road became their second home, a whirlwind of cityscapes, sold-out arenas, and the electric energy of live performance.

The band's live shows were a phenomenon unto themselves. Their infectious energy and undeniable chemistry on stage created an atmosphere of pure euphoria. Darius Rucker's soulful vocals, coupled with Mark Bryan's melodic guitar riffs, ignited the crowd, transforming concert venues into a sea of swaying bodies and sing-alongs.

As Hootie & the Blowfish's popularity soared, so did the scale of their tours. What began as intimate club shows transformed into massive stadium spectacles. The band's ability to connect with their audience on a personal level, even in the face of overwhelming crowds, was a testament to their genuine warmth and charisma.

Touring was a double-edged sword. While it provided the band with a platform to share their music with millions of fans, it also took a toll on their personal lives. The constant travel, the grueling schedule, and the relentless demands of fame put a strain on their relationships and mental health.

Despite the challenges, the band persevered, driven by their passion for performing and the unwavering support of their fans. They found ways to balance their professional commitments with their personal lives, creating a sense of normalcy amidst the chaos.

The band's popularity extended far beyond the music industry. They became cultural icons, their image synonymous with youthful optimism and the spirit of the 1990s. Their music provided a soundtrack for countless life milestones, from high school graduations to weddings and everything in between.

As Hootie & the Blowfish continued to tour, they expanded their reach beyond the United States, captivating audiences around the world. Their music transcended language and cultural barriers, connecting with people on a universal level.

The band's ability to maintain their popularity throughout the years is a testament to their enduring appeal. Their music has stood the test of time, continuing to resonate with new generations of fans.

Chapter 4: Balancing Success And Personal Life

The meteoric rise of Hootie & the Blowfish thrust Darius Rucker into the blinding spotlight of fame. The transition from college life to global stardom was a seismic shift, demanding a delicate balancing act between personal fulfillment and the relentless demands of the music industry.

The intoxicating allure of success was a double-edged sword. On one hand, it offered unparalleled opportunities, creative freedom, and the ability to connect with millions of fans. On the other, it presented a myriad of challenges that tested the foundations of relationships, personal identity, and mental well-being.

Rucker, like many other celebrities, found himself navigating a complex labyrinth of public scrutiny. Every move was dissected, analyzed, and judged by the world at large. The constant pressure to maintain a flawless public image took its toll on his personal life, as he struggled to define himself beyond the persona of the rock star.

The demands of touring were particularly grueling. Endless nights on the road, away from family and friends, created a sense of isolation and detachment. The constant exposure to the intoxicating energy of live performance made it difficult to ground himself in reality. Rucker, like his bandmates, faced the challenge of maintaining a sense of normalcy amidst the whirlwind of fame.

Amidst the chaos, Rucker sought solace in his personal life. Marriage and family provided a grounding force, a sanctuary from the relentless demands of the music industry. His wife, Beth Leonard, became his rock, offering unwavering support and understanding. Together, they navigated the complexities of their lives, creating a sense of stability in a world that often felt chaotic.

The birth of their children brought a new perspective to Rucker's life. Fatherhood became a source of immense joy and fulfillment, grounding him in the present moment and reminding him of what truly mattered. The experience of raising a family helped him to prioritize his personal life, setting boundaries and creating a sense of balance.

However, balancing success and personal life was an ongoing challenge. The allure of the music industry, with its constant temptations and distractions, posed a constant threat to Rucker's relationships and well-being. It required unwavering commitment and self-discipline to maintain a sense of equilibrium.

Through it all, Rucker emerged as a resilient and determined individual. He learned to set boundaries, to prioritize his family, and to find moments of peace amidst the chaos. His ability to navigate the complexities of fame while maintaining his personal integrity is a testament to his character and strength.

The Challenges Of Fame

The ascent to stardom is a seductive siren song, promising wealth, adoration, and creative freedom. Yet, beneath the glittering facade lies a complex web of challenges that can test the mettle of even the most resilient individuals. Darius Rucker, like countless others who have achieved the pinnacle of celebrity, experienced firsthand the intoxicating highs and crushing lows of fame.

One of the most formidable challenges is the erosion of privacy. The once-ordinary life, filled with familiar routines and intimate connections, is replaced by a constant state of surveillance. Every move, every word, every action becomes fodder for public consumption. The loss of anonymity can be a profound and isolating experience.

Moreover, the intense pressure to maintain a flawless public image can be a suffocating burden. The fear of making mistakes, of disappointing fans, or of being judged harshly can lead to crippling anxiety. The constant scrutiny can distort one's sense of self, creating a chasm between the public persona and the private individual.

Another significant challenge is the manipulation of relationships. The allure of fame can attract a coterie of individuals whose motives are often questionable. Friendships and romantic partnerships are tested as people's priorities shift and allegiances are questioned. The constant influx of new acquaintances can make it difficult to discern genuine connections from superficial ones.

The psychological toll of fame cannot be overstated. The constant adrenaline rush of live performances, the relentless travel, and the lack of downtime can lead to burnout and exhaustion. The pressure to constantly exceed expectations can create a sense of never being good enough, fostering feelings of inadequacy and self-doubt.

Isolation is another insidious consequence of fame. As the circle of trusted confidantes shrinks, a sense of loneliness can creep in. The superficiality of many interactions can leave one yearning for genuine connection. The fear of being judged or misunderstood can create a barrier, making it difficult to form authentic relationships.

Despite the challenges, many individuals find a way to navigate the complexities of fame with grace and resilience. By setting boundaries, cultivating strong support systems, and maintaining a grounded perspective, it is possible to find balance and fulfillment.

Family Life and Relationships

Amidst the whirlwind of fame and fortune, Darius Rucker has managed to cultivate a sense of normalcy and prioritize his family life. Marriage and fatherhood have been anchors of stability, providing a sanctuary from the relentless demands of the music industry.

Rucker's wife, Beth Leonard, has been an unwavering source of support and love. Their partnership has weathered the storms of celebrity, serving as a testament to their enduring bond. Beth has been instrumental in creating a nurturing home environment for their children, shielding them from the intrusive glare of the spotlight.

The arrival of children brought an unparalleled joy to Rucker's life. Fatherhood has grounded him, offering a profound sense of purpose and fulfillment. The experience of raising children has instilled in him a deep appreciation for the simple pleasures of life, creating a healthy counterbalance to the fast-paced world of entertainment.

Juggling the demands of a demanding career with the responsibilities of family life has been a constant challenge. Countless hours spent on the road, away from loved ones, have tested the strength of their relationships. However, Rucker and his family have developed strategies to maintain a strong connection, even in the face of separation. Technology has played a crucial role in bridging the physical distance, allowing them to stay connected and share precious moments.

The Rucker family has made a conscious effort to live a relatively private life. While they understand the inherent nature of their public personas, they have worked diligently to protect their children from the intrusive glare of the spotlight. By creating a nurturing and supportive home environment, they have fostered a sense of normalcy and security for their family.

Balancing the demands of fame with the desire to provide a stable and loving home for his children has been a delicate balancing act. Rucker has learned the importance of setting boundaries and prioritizing family time. He has made a conscious effort to be present in his children's lives, participating in their activities and creating lasting memories.

The challenges of maintaining a strong family unit in the face of public scrutiny are immense. However, Rucker and his family have demonstrated resilience and determination. Their love for one another has been the cornerstone of their relationship, enabling them to navigate the complexities of their lives with grace and dignity.

Chapter 5: Beyond the Hits

While Darius Rucker is undoubtedly celebrated for his chart-topping hits and infectious melodies, his artistry extends far beyond the realm of radio-friendly anthems. Beneath the surface of the country music superstar lies a versatile musician with a deep appreciation for various musical genres and a desire to explore the depths of his creative potential.

Rucker's roots in gospel music have continued to influence his work, imbuing his songs with a soulful depth and spiritual resonance. His ability to seamlessly blend traditional country elements with gospel inflections has created a unique and captivating sound. Tracks like "Alright" showcase this fusion, demonstrating his versatility as an artist.

Beyond his country music endeavors, Rucker has also dabbled in other genres, showcasing his musical range. His collaboration with the rock band Hootie & the

Blowfish is a testament to his ability to adapt to different musical styles. The band's blend of rock, pop, and folk elements showcased Rucker's vocal prowess and his capacity to connect with a diverse audience.

Moreover, Rucker's songwriting abilities extend beyond the confines of commercial success. His lyrics often delve into personal experiences, exploring themes of love, loss, and the complexities of human relationships. Songs like "This" and "It Won't Be Like This For Long" showcase his ability to craft heartfelt and relatable narratives.

As an artist, Rucker has demonstrated a willingness to take risks and experiment with new sounds. His collaborations with other musicians, such as his work with Luke Bryan on "Neon Moon," have allowed him to explore different musical territories and expand his fanbase.

Beyond the studio, Rucker's live performances are a testament to his passion for music and his ability to connect with audiences on a profound level. His energetic stage presence and soulful vocals create an unforgettable experience for fans of all ages.

Darius Rucker's artistry extends far beyond the realm of commercial success. His ability to seamlessly blend genres, explore different musical avenues, and connect with audiences on a deep emotional level has solidified his status as a true musician. As he continues to evolve as an artist, it is clear that there is still much to discover in the world of Darius Rucker.

Other Albums and Musical Explorations

Beyond the commercial triumphs and chart-topping singles, Darius Rucker's discography reveals a multifaceted artist eager to explore the depths of his musicality. His subsequent albums offer a glimpse into his evolving sound and artistic aspirations.

Following the meteoric success of "Cracked Rear View," Hootie & the Blowfish released several albums that showcased their continued growth and evolution. While not achieving the same commercial heights as their debut, these albums offered a deeper dive into the band's songwriting and musicianship.

Tracks like "Time" and "Old Man and Me" showcased a more mature and introspective side to the band, demonstrating their ability to evolve beyond the confines of their initial sound.

Rucker's solo career has also been marked by a willingness to experiment and explore different musical territories. Albums like "Charleston, South Carolina 1966" and "True Believers" showcased his roots in soul and R&B, paying homage to the musical influences that shaped his artistry. These projects allowed him to connect with his heritage and showcase a different facet of his vocal range.

Moreover, Rucker has embraced the opportunity to collaborate with other artists, expanding his musical horizons. His collaborations with artists from different genres have resulted in unexpected and refreshing musical fusions. These collaborations have not only introduced Rucker to new audiences but have also allowed him to experiment with different sounds and styles.

Rucker's discography is a testament to his enduring passion for music and his commitment to artistic growth. While commercial success is undoubtedly important, it is evident that his primary motivation is to create music that resonates with his soul and connects with his audience on a deeper level.

The Band's Evolution

Hootie & the Blowfish were more than just a band; they were a cultural phenomenon that captured the hearts of millions. Their journey from a college garage band to international stardom was marked by a remarkable evolution, both musically and personally.

The release of "Cracked Rear View" catapulted the band into the stratosphere of pop culture, but it was their ability to adapt and grow that ensured their longevity. As the years passed, Hootie & the Blowfish experimented with different sounds and styles, exploring the boundaries of their musical identity. They delved deeper into storytelling, incorporating more complex arrangements and lyrical themes into their music.

The band members' personal growth also influenced their artistic direction. As they matured, their perspectives on life and relationships evolved, and these experiences found their way into their songwriting. The music became more introspective and reflective, reflecting the complexities of the human experience.

While the band's commercial success may have declined in subsequent albums, their artistic integrity remained intact. They refused to compromise their vision for the sake of commercial gain, choosing instead to create music that resonated with their souls. This unwavering commitment to authenticity earned them the respect of their fans and solidified their status as respected musicians.

Hootie & the Blowfish's evolution was also marked by a growing sense of social consciousness. They used their platform to raise awareness about important issues and to give back to their community. Their philanthropic endeavors and involvement in charitable causes demonstrated their commitment to making a positive impact on the world.

Ultimately, Hootie & the Blowfish's legacy extends far beyond their chart-topping hits. Their journey from college friends to seasoned musicians is a testament to the power of perseverance, creativity, and friendship. The band's evolution serves as an inspiration to aspiring artists, demonstrating that artistic growth and longevity are possible even in the face of immense commercial success.

PART III

SOLO CAREER AND COUNTRY MUSIC

Chapter 6: The Decision To Go Solo

For years, Darius Rucker had been the charismatic frontman of Hootie & the Blowfish, a band that had captured the hearts of millions. The intoxicating rush of fame, the camaraderie of shared dreams, and the thrill of live performance had defined a significant chapter of his life. Yet, beneath the surface of this seemingly idyllic existence, a growing sense of artistic restlessness and a yearning for a new challenge began to emerge.

The decision to embark on a solo career was not made lightly. It was a leap of faith, a calculated risk that required immense courage and self-belief. The comforts of a successful band, with its established fanbase and proven formula, were undeniably alluring. However, Rucker's creative spirit yearned for new horizons, a chance to explore uncharted musical territory.

The desire to exercise greater artistic control was a driving force behind his decision. As the lead vocalist of Hootie & the Blowfish, Rucker's talent was undoubtedly a cornerstone of the band's success. However, the collaborative nature of the band dynamic limited his ability to fully express his artistic vision. A solo career offered the opportunity to be the sole architect of his musical world, to shape every aspect of his sound and message.

Furthermore, the allure of a fresh start was undeniably enticing. The opportunity to reinvent himself, to shed the image of the rock frontman and embrace a new musical identity, was a prospect that filled Rucker with excitement and anticipation. He was eager to challenge himself, to prove his versatility as an artist, and to connect with a new audience.

The decision to leave the band was undoubtedly a difficult one, filled with mixed emotions. The bonds of friendship forged during their years together were deep and enduring. However, Rucker realized that personal and artistic growth often requires making tough choices. With a heavy heart but a determined spirit, he embarked on a new chapter in his musical journey.

Reasons For Leaving Hootie & The Blowfish

Darius Rucker's decision to step away from Hootie & the Blowfish was a pivotal moment in his career. The band had achieved extraordinary success, but beneath the glittering facade of fame, a complex interplay of factors influenced Rucker's choice.

A primary catalyst was the desire for artistic evolution. While Hootie & the Blowfish enjoyed immense popularity, Rucker yearned to explore new musical territories and express his creativity in a different light. The confines of a successful band, though comfortable, limited his artistic freedom. The allure of solo artistry, with its promise of greater autonomy and creative control, became increasingly compelling.

Moreover, the relentless demands of touring and the pressures of maintaining a public persona took a toll on Rucker's personal life. The constant travel, coupled with the intense scrutiny that comes with fame, created an imbalance between his professional and personal life. He yearned for a more grounded existence, one that would allow him to spend more time with his family and pursue other interests.

The desire to challenge himself and step outside of his comfort zone was another significant factor. Rucker possessed a deep-seated ambition to prove his versatility as an artist. By embarking on a solo career, he had the opportunity to showcase a different side of his musicality and connect with a new audience.

Furthermore, the natural progression of a band's lifecycle played a role in Rucker's decision. After achieving unprecedented success, it can be challenging to maintain the same level of creative energy and momentum. The desire to explore new avenues and avoid stagnation became a compelling force.

Ultimately, Rucker's decision to leave Hootie & the Blowfish was a culmination of various factors. The desire for artistic growth, the need for a more balanced personal life, and the allure of new challenges converged to create a perfect storm that propelled him towards a solo career. It was a bold and risky move, but one that would ultimately redefine his musical journey.

Transitioning to Country Music

Darius Rucker's decision to venture into country music was a bold and unexpected move that defied conventional wisdom. After achieving unprecedented success as the frontman of Hootie & the Blowfish, a band synonymous with the rock and pop genres, the prospect of transitioning to a decidedly different musical landscape was fraught with both excitement and uncertainty.

The decision to pursue a country music career was rooted in Rucker's deep-seated love for the genre. Growing up in the South, he had been exposed to the rich tapestry of country music, from the classic sounds of Merle Haggard and George Jones to the contemporary hits of the 90s. The genre's storytelling tradition, combined with its emotional depth, resonated profoundly with him.

However, the transition was far from seamless. The country music world was a distinct ecosystem with its own established stars and traditions. Skepticism and doubt were prevalent as Rucker, a seasoned rock star, ventured into this unfamiliar territory. Critics questioned his authenticity and wondered if he could truly connect with the core country audience.

To overcome these challenges, Rucker immersed himself in the country music scene. He spent countless hours listening to classic country records, studying the nuances of the genre, and honing his songwriting skills. He surrounded himself with talented Nashville musicians and producers, eager to learn from their expertise.

Rucker's soulful voice, a hallmark of his career, proved to be a valuable asset in his transition to country music. His ability to infuse his songs with raw emotion and authenticity resonated with country fans, who embraced his unique blend of rock and country influences.

The release of his debut country album, "Learn to Live," marked a pivotal moment in his career. The album was a critical and commercial success, solidifying Rucker's status as a bona fide country star. Songs like "Don't" and "Alright" became instant classics, showcasing his ability to seamlessly blend traditional country elements with contemporary sensibilities.

Transitioning from rock to country music was undoubtedly a risky endeavor, but Darius Rucker's unwavering belief in his talent, coupled with his willingness to embrace new challenges, paved the way for his success. His journey serves as an inspiration to aspiring artists, proving that with passion, perseverance, and a genuine love for music, it is possible to transcend genre boundaries and achieve extraordinary success.

Chapter 7: Breaking Into Country Music

Darius Rucker's transition from the rock frontman of Hootie & the Blowfish to a country music superstar was a bold and unprecedented move. It was a leap of faith into a genre with its own established stars and traditions, where skepticism and doubt were as prevalent as the twang of steel guitars.

Rucker's decision to pursue a country music career was rooted in a genuine love for the genre. Growing up in the South, he had been immersed in the rich tapestry of country music, from the classic sounds of Merle Haggard and George Jones to the contemporary hits of the 90s. The storytelling tradition, the emotional depth, and the connection to his roots resonated deeply with him.

However, breaking into the country music scene was no easy feat. As a newcomer, with a rock star past, Rucker faced a steep uphill climb. He had to prove his authenticity, his understanding of the genre, and his ability to connect with the core country audience. The weight of expectations, both from the industry and the fans, was immense.

To overcome these challenges, Rucker immersed himself in the country music world. He spent countless hours listening to classic country records, studying the nuances of the genre, and honing his songwriting skills. He surrounded himself with talented Nashville musicians and producers, eager to learn from their expertise.

Rucker's soulful voice, a hallmark of his career, proved to be a valuable asset in his transition to country music. His ability to infuse his songs with raw emotion and authenticity resonated with country fans. He found a way to bridge the gap between his rock background and the traditional country sound, creating a unique and compelling style.

The release of his debut country album, "Learn to Live," was a pivotal moment. The album's lead single, "Don't Think I Don't Think About It," climbed to the top of the country charts, making Rucker the first Black artist to do so since Charley Pride in 1983. This groundbreaking achievement shattered stereotypes and opened doors for other artists of color.

Breaking into country music was a challenging but ultimately rewarding journey for Darius Rucker. His determination, talent, and unwavering belief in himself allowed him to overcome obstacles and establish himself as a respected and beloved figure in the genre. His success paved the way for other artists, demonstrating that country music is a space for diverse voices and perspectives.

Early Country Singles And Challenges

Darius Rucker's foray into country music was marked by both triumphs and challenges. While his transition from rock to country was met with skepticism by some, his undeniable talent and charisma quickly began to win over audiences.

His debut country single, "Don't Think I Don't Think About It," was a watershed moment. The song, a poignant ballad about heartbreak and longing, resonated deeply with country music fans. Its success was a testament to Rucker's ability to connect with audiences on an emotional level. The song climbed to the top of the country charts, making history as the first number-one country single by a Black artist since Charley Pride in 1983.

The success of "Don't Think I Don't Think About It" was followed by a string of chart-topping hits, including "It Won't Be Like This For Long" and "Alright." These songs solidified Rucker's position as a rising star in the country music world and showcased his versatility as an artist. His ability to seamlessly blend traditional country elements with contemporary pop sensibilities proved to be a winning formula.

However, the path to country music stardom was not without its obstacles. Rucker faced skepticism and doubt from some quarters of the country music industry. There were those who questioned his authenticity and wondered if he could truly connect with the core country audience. Overcoming these preconceived notions required unwavering determination and a steadfast belief in his own abilities.

Building a new fanbase in a genre dominated by established stars was a daunting task. Rucker had to prove himself as a songwriter, performer, and entertainer. He spent countless hours honing his craft, immersing himself in the country music tradition, and connecting with fans on a personal level.

Despite the challenges, Rucker's early country singles were a resounding success. They not only showcased his talent but also helped to break down barriers and expand the definition of country music. His journey served as an inspiration to aspiring artists, proving that with hard work, dedication, and a genuine love for music, it is possible to achieve success in any genre.

First Country Album And Its Impact

Darius Rucker's debut country album, *Learn to Live*, marked a pivotal moment in his career. It was a bold statement of intent, a declaration that he was serious about making a lasting impact on the country music landscape. Released in 2008, the album was a critical and commercial success, solidifying Rucker's position as a rising star in the genre.

Learn to Live was a carefully curated collection of songs that showcased Rucker's soulful vocals and his ability to connect with the heart of country music. The album seamlessly blended traditional country elements with contemporary pop sensibilities, creating a sound that was both familiar and refreshing. Tracks like "Don't Think I Don't Think About It," "It Won't Be Like This For Long," and "Alright" became instant classics, dominating the country charts and earning Rucker widespread acclaim.

The album's success was a testament to Rucker's unwavering belief in his talent and his ability to connect with audiences on a deep emotional level. It defied expectations and shattered stereotypes, proving that a Black artist could achieve mainstream success in country music. *Learn to Live* not only introduced Rucker to a new generation of fans but also expanded the boundaries of the genre, demonstrating that country music could be inclusive and diverse.

Beyond the commercial success, *Learn to Live* had a profound impact on the country music industry. It challenged the status quo and opened doors for other artists of color. Rucker's breakthrough paved the way for a more inclusive and diverse country music scene, inspiring countless musicians to pursue their dreams without fear of rejection.

The album's success also solidified Rucker's position as a crossover artist. His ability to bridge the gap between rock and country music expanded the genre's appeal to a wider audience. *Learn to Live* was a watershed moment, not only for Rucker's career but for the entire country music industry. It marked the beginning of a new era, one characterized by inclusivity, diversity, and a willingness to embrace change.

Chapter 8: Country Music Success

Darius Rucker's journey into country music was a bold gamble that paid off in spades. His transition from rock frontman to country superstar was a testament to his talent, resilience, and unwavering belief in himself. The success he achieved was a combination of hard work, strategic positioning, and a genuine connection with his audience.

Rucker's breakthrough came with his debut country album, *Learn to Live*, and its lead single, "Don't Think I Don't Think About It." This song not only topped the country charts but also shattered barriers, making Rucker the first Black artist to reach number one since Charley Pride. The success of this album and its subsequent singles catapulted him into the upper echelon of country music stardom.

What set Rucker apart was his ability to bridge the gap between traditional country and contemporary pop. His soulful vocals and heartfelt delivery resonated with both longtime country fans and a new generation of listeners. He brought a fresh perspective to the genre while honoring its rich history.

Rucker's success was also due to his authentic connection with his audience. He was genuine, relatable, and possessed a down-to-earth charm that made him endearing to fans. His ability to tell stories through his music created a deep emotional connection that transcended the boundaries of the genre.

Beyond the music, Rucker became a symbol of diversity and inclusion in country music. His success challenged stereotypes and paved the way for other artists of color to find their place in the genre. He proved that country music could be a welcoming space for a wide range of voices and perspectives.

Rucker's journey from rock star to country music icon is a testament to the power of perseverance and belief in oneself. His success has inspired countless artists to pursue their dreams, regardless of the odds. He has become a beloved figure in the country music world, and his legacy will continue to inspire future generations.

Chart-Topping Hits and Awards

Darius Rucker's ascent to country music stardom was marked by a string of chart-topping hits that solidified his status as a dominant force in the genre. His ability to craft catchy melodies and heartfelt lyrics resonated with audiences on a profound level, propelling him to the top of the country music charts.

Songs like "Don't Think I Don't Think About It," "It Won't Be Like This For Long," and "Alright" became instant classics, defining a new era of country music. These songs showcased Rucker's vocal prowess and his ability to connect with listeners on an emotional level. His music transcended generational divides, appealing to both longtime country fans and a younger demographic.

Rucker's success extended beyond chart positions. His albums consistently achieved platinum and multi-platinum status, a testament to his enduring popularity.

He sold out arenas across the country, drawing massive crowds eager to experience his live performances.

In recognition of his contributions to the music industry, Rucker has received numerous awards and accolades. He has been honored by the Country Music Association (CMA), the Academy of Country Music (ACM), and the Grammy Awards. His win for the New Artist Award at the CMA Awards made history, as he was the first Black artist to receive this honor.

Rucker's ability to consistently deliver chart-topping hits and garner critical acclaim is a testament to his talent, hard work, and unwavering dedication to his craft. His success has not only solidified his position as a country music superstar but has also inspired countless artists to pursue their dreams.

Establishing Himself As A Country Star

Darius Rucker's journey from rock frontman to country music superstar was nothing short of remarkable. With a blend of raw talent, unwavering determination, and a genuine connection with his audience, he successfully established himself as a dominant force in the genre.

Beyond the chart-topping hits and critical acclaim, Rucker's ability to connect with fans on a personal level was instrumental in solidifying his status as a country star. His down-to-earth demeanor, coupled with his heartfelt lyrics, resonated with audiences of all ages. He was more than just a singer; he was a storyteller, painting vivid pictures of life, love, and loss.

Rucker's live performances were legendary. His energetic stage presence and powerful vocals captivated audiences, creating an unforgettable concert experience. He had an uncanny ability to connect with the crowd, making each show feel like an intimate gathering.

As his popularity grew, Rucker became a sought-after collaborator. He worked with a diverse range of artists, from established country stars to rising newcomers. These collaborations helped to expand his fanbase and introduce his music to new audiences.

Moreover, Rucker's philanthropic efforts solidified his reputation as a genuine and caring individual. His involvement in various charitable causes endeared him to fans and earned him respect within the industry.

Establishing oneself as a country star requires more than just musical talent. It demands a strong work ethic, resilience, and a deep understanding of the genre. Darius Rucker possessed all of these qualities in abundance. His journey from rock to country music was a testament to his versatility and determination, inspiring countless artists to pursue their dreams.

PART IV

BEYOND THE MUSIC

Chapter 9: Philanthropy And Activism

Beyond his musical accomplishments, Darius Rucker has established himself as a dedicated philanthropist and advocate for various causes. His commitment to giving back to the community is as evident as his talent for songwriting.

Rucker's philanthropic endeavors often intersect with his musical career. He has leveraged his platform to raise awareness and funds for numerous charitable organizations. His involvement in causes such as education, healthcare, and children's welfare reflects his deep-rooted desire to make a positive impact on the world.

One of Rucker's most significant philanthropic contributions is his work with the Hootie & the Blowfish Foundation. Established by the band, the foundation supports a variety of causes, including education, homelessness, and environmental conservation. Rucker has been a tireless advocate for the foundation, using his influence to raise millions of dollars for these important initiatives.

Additionally, Rucker has been involved in numerous other charitable endeavors. He has supported organizations focused on cancer research, disaster relief, and veterans' affairs. His willingness to lend his name and time to worthy causes has inspired countless fans to get involved in their own communities.

Rucker's philanthropic work extends beyond financial contributions. He has actively participated in fundraising events, volunteer initiatives, and awareness campaigns. His genuine commitment to making a difference has earned him the respect and admiration of his fans and peers alike.

Beyond philanthropy, Rucker has also used his platform to address social issues. He has spoken out on topics such as racial equality and education reform, using his influence to promote positive change. His willingness to use his voice to advocate for important causes has solidified his status as a role model and a leader in the entertainment industry.

Rucker's commitment to philanthropy and activism is an integral part of his legacy. His dedication to giving back has inspired countless individuals to make a difference in their own communities. By using his platform for good, he has shown that celebrities can be powerful forces for positive change.

Charitable Endeavors and Community Involvement

Darius Rucker's commitment to giving back to his community is as profound as his musical talent. Beyond the glitz and glamor of the entertainment industry, he has consistently demonstrated a genuine desire to make a positive impact on the world. His philanthropic endeavors have touched countless lives and solidified his reputation as a role model and a humanitarian.

One of Rucker's most significant contributions has been his work with the Hootie & the Blowfish Foundation. Founded by the band, the foundation supports a wide range of causes, including education, homelessness, and environmental conservation.

Rucker has been a tireless advocate for the organization, leveraging his celebrity status to raise awareness and funds for its initiatives. The foundation's focus on education is particularly close to Rucker's heart, reflecting his belief in the transformative power of education to break cycles of poverty and create opportunities for young people.

In addition to his work with the Hootie & the Blowfish Foundation, Rucker has supported numerous other charitable organizations. He has been a vocal supporter of cancer research, participating in fundraising events and raising awareness about the importance of early detection.

Rucker has also been involved in disaster relief efforts, providing aid to communities affected by natural disasters. His philanthropic endeavors extend beyond financial contributions, as he has actively participated in volunteer work and community outreach programs.

Rucker's commitment to giving back is rooted in his own upbringing. He understands the challenges faced by many people and is determined to use his platform to make a difference. His philanthropic work is an inspiration to his fans, demonstrating that even the most famous people can find time to give back to their communities.

By combining his musical talent with his philanthropic efforts, Darius Rucker has created a powerful legacy. His dedication to making the world a better place has solidified his status as a role model and a true humanitarian.

Advocacy For Social Causes

Beyond his musical talents and philanthropic endeavors, Darius Rucker has emerged as a vocal advocate for several social causes. Leveraging his platform as a public figure, he has used his voice to raise awareness and drive positive change.

Rucker has been a consistent supporter of education reform. Recognizing the transformative power of education, he has dedicated significant time and resources to initiatives aimed at improving access to quality education for all children.

His work with the Hootie & the Blowfish Foundation, which focuses on education-related programs, underscores his commitment to this cause. Through his advocacy, Rucker has inspired countless individuals to become involved in educational initiatives and to support policies that prioritize student success.

Additionally, Rucker has been a vocal advocate for racial equality. As a Black man who has achieved significant success in the predominantly white world of country music, he is uniquely positioned to address issues of discrimination and prejudice.

He has used his platform to speak out against racism and to promote unity and understanding. Rucker's willingness to use his voice to address sensitive and challenging issues has made him a role model for others, inspiring them to stand up for what they believe in.

Furthermore, Rucker has shown a deep commitment to environmental causes. Recognizing the importance of protecting the planet for future generations, he has supported initiatives aimed at conservation and sustainability. His involvement in environmental organizations and his public statements on climate change have helped to raise awareness of this critical issue.

By using his platform to advocate for social causes, Darius Rucker has demonstrated that celebrities can be powerful forces for positive change. His commitment to education, racial equality, and environmental protection has inspired countless individuals to get involved in their communities and to make a difference in the world.

Chapter 10: Business Ventures And Other Interests

Beyond his music career, Darius Rucker has demonstrated a keen business acumen and a diverse range of interests. His entrepreneurial spirit and ability to identify opportunities have led him to explore various ventures outside of the entertainment industry.

One of Rucker's notable business ventures is his involvement in the restaurant industry. With a passion for food and hospitality, he has opened several successful restaurants, offering patrons a taste of Southern cuisine and a welcoming atmosphere. These establishments have become popular destinations, drawing in both locals and tourists alike.

Rucker's business ventures extend beyond the culinary world. He has also invested in various other enterprises, showcasing his entrepreneurial spirit and willingness to explore new opportunities. His ability to identify promising ventures and build successful partnerships has enabled him to diversify his income streams and create financial stability for himself and his family.

In addition to his business endeavors, Rucker has a passion for golf. He is a skilled golfer and has participated in several celebrity golf tournaments. His love for the sport has led to various endorsements and sponsorships, further expanding his business interests.

Rucker's ability to balance his music career with his entrepreneurial pursuits is a testament to his drive and determination. He has successfully created a diversified portfolio that ensures financial security while allowing him to pursue his passions. His entrepreneurial spirit serves as an inspiration to others, demonstrating that success in one field can be leveraged to create opportunities in other areas.

Entrepreneurship and Business Ventures

Beyond the glitz and glamor of the music industry, Darius Rucker has proven himself to be a savvy entrepreneur with a keen business acumen. His ability to identify opportunities and build successful ventures has solidified his status as a multifaceted and influential figure.

Rucker's entrepreneurial journey began with his involvement in the restaurant industry. With a passion for food and hospitality, he opened several successful eateries that have become popular destinations for both locals and tourists alike. His restaurants are known for their warm atmosphere, delicious cuisine, and a touch of Southern charm. By leveraging his celebrity status and business savvy, Rucker has created thriving establishments that extend his brand beyond the music industry.

Rucker has diversified his business portfolio by investing in various other enterprises. His keen eye for opportunity and ability to identify promising ventures have allowed him to build a substantial business empire. From real estate to technology, Rucker has demonstrated a willingness to explore different industries and take calculated risks.

Rucker's entrepreneurial spirit is driven by a desire for financial security and independence. By building a diverse portfolio of businesses, he has created a solid foundation for himself and his family. His success in the business world is a testament to his hard work, determination, and ability to adapt to changing circumstances.

Moreover, Rucker's entrepreneurial endeavors have allowed him to create job opportunities for others. By investing in local businesses and communities, he has contributed to economic growth and development. His commitment to giving back extends beyond charitable donations and includes creating employment opportunities for people in the communities he serves.

Darius Rucker's success as an entrepreneur is a testament to his versatility and business acumen. His ability to balance his music career with his entrepreneurial pursuits is an inspiration to aspiring business owners and musicians alike. By demonstrating that it is possible to achieve success in multiple fields, Rucker has become a role model for a new generation of entrepreneurs.

Hobbies And Passions Outside Of Music

Beyond the world of music, Darius Rucker possesses a diverse range of interests and hobbies that enrich his life. These pursuits offer him a much-needed respite from the demands of his music career and provide a sense of balance and fulfillment.

One of Rucker's most prominent passions is sports. A dedicated fan of both college and professional football, he has often expressed his love for the game. His enthusiasm for sports has led to various collaborations and endorsements, allowing him to combine his passion with his professional life.

Golf is another sport that Rucker enjoys. He is a skilled golfer and has participated in numerous celebrity golf tournaments. The sport provides him with an opportunity to relax, compete, and spend quality time with friends.

Rucker also has a keen interest in the culinary arts. His passion for food is evident in his successful restaurant ventures. Cooking and entertaining friends and family at home is a hobby he greatly enjoys. It allows him to explore different flavors and create memorable dining experiences.

In addition to his love for sports, food, and entertainment, Rucker is also a devoted family man. Spending quality time with his loved ones is a top priority for him. Whether it's attending his children's sporting events, going on family vacations, or simply relaxing at home, Rucker cherishes these moments and finds great joy in his role as a husband and father.

Rucker's diverse interests contribute to his well-rounded personality and provide a refreshing counterbalance to the fast-paced world of music. His ability to find fulfillment and enjoyment in various aspects of life is a testament to his ability to live a balanced and fulfilling life.

Chapter 11: Legacy And Impact

Darius Rucker's impact on music and culture extends far beyond his chart-topping hits and sold-out concerts. His career has been marked by a series of groundbreaking achievements that have reshaped the landscape of both country music and popular culture as a whole.

As a Black artist who successfully transitioned from rock to country music, Rucker has been a trailblazer and a role model. His groundbreaking success shattered stereotypes and opened doors for other artists of color to pursue their dreams in a genre that was traditionally dominated by white performers. His journey has helped to diversify country music and make it more inclusive, reflecting the changing demographics of America.

Rucker's music has also had a profound impact on popular culture. His ability to blend traditional country elements with contemporary pop sensibilities created a new sound that resonated with a wide audience. His songs have become anthems for love, loss, and heartbreak, providing a soundtrack for countless life experiences.

Beyond his musical influence, Rucker has also made a significant impact on philanthropy and social activism. His commitment to giving back to his community and using his platform to address important issues has inspired countless others to get involved in making the world a better place.

Rucker's career serves as a testament to the power of perseverance, talent, and authenticity. He has proven that with hard work and dedication, it is possible to overcome obstacles and achieve extraordinary success. His influence on music and culture will continue to be felt for generations to come.

Enduring Popularity And Fan Base

One of the most remarkable aspects of Darius Rucker's career is his enduring popularity. While many artists experience fleeting fame, Rucker has managed to maintain a strong and dedicated fan base throughout his career. This enduring popularity is a testament to his talent, versatility, and genuine connection with his audience.

Rucker's ability to transcend genres has been a key factor in his sustained success. His journey from rock frontman to country music superstar has broadened his appeal, attracting fans from diverse musical backgrounds. This crossover success has allowed him to build a loyal and dedicated following that spans generations.

Moreover, Rucker's music has a timeless quality that resonates with listeners of all ages. His songs often explore universal themes of love, loss, and hope, which connect with people on a deep emotional level. This ability to tap into the human experience has ensured that his music remains relevant and enduring.

Rucker's philanthropic endeavors and his commitment to giving back to the community have also contributed to his enduring popularity. Fans appreciate his genuine desire to make a positive impact on the world, and his philanthropic work has solidified his reputation as a role model.

The live concert experience has been instrumental in maintaining Rucker's connection with his fans. His energetic performances and charismatic stage presence create an unforgettable experience that keeps audiences coming back for more. The intimate connection he fosters with his fans during live shows has deepened his bond with them and solidified his status as a beloved performer.

In an era of rapidly changing musical tastes, Darius Rucker's ability to maintain a strong and dedicated fanbase is a testament to his artistry and his genuine connection with his audience. His enduring popularity is a testament to the power of music to transcend time and connect people on a profound level.

CONCLUSION

A Legacy Defined by Versatility and Impact

Darius Rucker's journey from the frontman of a rock band to a revered country music icon is a testament to his extraordinary talent, resilience, and unwavering determination. His career is a tapestry woven with threads of musical brilliance, philanthropic endeavors, and a genuine connection with his audience.

From the infectious energy of Hootie & the Blowfish to the soulful depth of his country music career, Rucker has consistently demonstrated a remarkable ability to adapt and evolve. His willingness to embrace new challenges and explore different musical genres has allowed him to connect with a diverse audience and solidify his status as a versatile and enduring artist.

Beyond his musical accomplishments, Rucker has emerged as a powerful force for positive change. His commitment to philanthropy, social activism, and community involvement has left an indelible mark on the world. By using his platform to advocate for important causes, he has inspired countless individuals to become involved in their communities and make a difference.

Rucker's impact on music and culture extends far beyond his chart-topping hits and sold-out concerts. He has broken down barriers, challenged stereotypes, and expanded the definition of what it means to be a country music star. His journey is a testament to the power of human spirit and the belief that with hard work, dedication, and a genuine connection with one's audience, it is possible to achieve extraordinary success.

As Darius Rucker continues to evolve as an artist and a philanthropist, his legacy will undoubtedly endure. His story is a source of inspiration for aspiring musicians, entrepreneurs, and humanitarians alike. He has proven that with talent, passion, and a commitment to making a difference, it is possible to achieve greatness and leave a lasting impact on the world.

Made in the USA
Coppell, TX
07 November 2024

39795285R00057